Encouragement

A Wife's
Special Gift

Ruth McRoberts Ward

BAKER BOOK HOUSE
Grand Rapids, Michigan 49516

Original art by Dean Vavak.
Book design by Ben Pirrone.

Copyright 1979 by
Baker Book House Company

ISBN: 0-8010-9698-9

Library of Congress
Card No. 77-79475

Printed in the United States of America

Dedicated to
the couples who have
come to us for help.

ACKNOWLEDGMENTS

The author gratefully acknowledges the kindness of authors and publishers in giving permission to quote from their works in this book.

Passages from *How to Have a Happy Marriage* by Dave and Vera Mace, copyright © 1977; from *Discovering Love* by Lance Webb, copyright © 1946; and from *Letters to Karen: On Keeping Love in Marriage* by Charlie W. Shedd, copyright © 1965 are used with the kind permission of Abingdon Press. Quotations from *Heaven Help the Home!* by Howard G. Hendricks, copyright © 1974 by Scripture Press Publications, are used by permission.

CONTENTS

INTRODUCTION

Two extreme cries — one for the equality of women and the other for a fervent, total submission to men — echo today. But do these concepts really clash?

Wives crave secure and satisfying marriages and long also to be fulfilled and happy as individuals. Must we women choose between these two desires?

Proverbs 18:22 says, *Whoso findeth a wife findeth a good thing.* Yet many husbands today honestly take exception to this teaching. For them, the biblical role model of the husband leading the family as head of the home and loving the wife as Christ loved the Church isn't working very well.

Why?

All couples at first have some problems of communication and adjustment. But in some marriages wives frantically search for answers while their husbands wait for solutions so they can live in peace without argument, hassle and fear of manipulation. But then as they understand why these difficulties surface and how common and normal such difficulties are, both husband and wife relax.

Sharing a life together is never simple; that's why a good marriage is priceless. And the key to a good marriage lies in a wife's special gift of encouragement — a God-given ability.

A husband desperately needs his wife's encouragement to supplement and draw out his potential strengths of leadership — the quality women yearn for in their men. So when the wife understands her strategic position in relation to her husband and accepts her unique place of encouragement in the marriage, the relationship with her husband will be headed toward the ideal situation — a good marriage where both partners realize personal worth.

I am delighted to share in these pages workable ideas about how a wife can encourage her husband to reach his potential and to become the type of husband she needs. These simple ideas on mending marriages — which my husband, Jim, and I have used over the past 23 years — have sweetened and strengthened many marriages, including our own.

In this book, we will discuss (1) what the major and minor tension areas are in most marriages, (2) how to anticipate these problems, and (3) how to deal graciously and wisely with them as soon as they arise, thereby avoiding unnecessary friction. And all this mending can take place without a professional counselor before a little tear becomes an ugly rip.

Since we women do most of this kind of reading, and most of the talking, too, this book is addressed to you, the wife, in hopes you'll lovingly pass it on to your husband in bits and pieces where it applies and as most men prefer to hear it.

Ruth Ward

Ruth Ward
York, Pennsylvania

1

HOW NOT TO PITCH A TENT

Did you ever watch a man erect a heavy camping tent? He struggles under the bulky, musty-smelling canvas to raise it overhead while at the same time trying to stabilize the wobbly center pole.

It's tough to handle an awkward tent alone. But with the right assistance, it's quite simple for the man in charge to set the center pole and then secure the outer edges. Building a strong and secure marriage is much like raising a tent. It involves struggle, naturally, but it becomes much easier with the right kind of encouragement.

Different marriages, like different kinds of tents, present different problems. And since no formula for success fits them all, it's helpful to observe what does and doesn't work for others.

SAGGY AND LOOSE

Some wives, upon learning that husbands are supposed to be heads of the home, are so eager to be in submission that they insist their husbands make all the decisions, even the little ones. These same wives say they want to be entirely dependent, yet they squirm restlessly under the apparent weaknesses and inabilities they observe in their husbands.

It is a very slow business getting this kind of tent up, because the husband wants and needs his wife's support and assistance. Yet, she holds back, afraid that she will overstep submission and be accused of leading. These tent dwellers are insecure because they live in indecision.

SLANTED AND LOPSIDED

Other wives, suspecting their husbands lack ambition and know-how, stand on the sidelines, watching their mates as they struggle to hoist the canvas overhead or to maneuver the center pole into place, and shout orders at them.

This domineering wife barks, "You're off center! Can't you hurry? It's getting dark. I thought you knew all about tents!"

Condescendingly, with a martyr's moan, she takes over—like a mother—and he becomes her assistant. For his benefit, she mutters "dummy" and broadcasts his inabilities to anyone who will listen.

Although misunderstood and underestimated, some husbands seem reasonably content with this setup. Unfortunately, others compensate by assuming extraordinary work loads, turning to alcohol or finding other away-from-home outlets.

Down deep, the wife doesn't really want to lead, and the husband sincerely wishes he could. But because of his lack of confidence and her disappointment, no one is ever really happy in this tent.

TOO TAUT

We've all seen the man who, determined to be the "head of the home," becomes arrogant and unyielding toward his wife. He forces her into subservience and quotes Scriptures on submission to justify his autocratic attitude.

This type of husband doesn't realize how much he needs the loving encouragement and ideas of his wife rather than her unwilling obedience. And she, denied any right of opinion or freedom of expression in the home, develops feelings of fear and resentment toward her husband.

This tent is pulled so tightly, it rips; the family inside is very tense and under constant strain.

WOBBLY CENTER POLE

This approach is new to me, but a trend today. The husband is declared the sole leader of the home, whether he wants to be or not and whether he's a Christian or not. He alone bears all the responsibility for himself, his wife and children.

The wife's only responsibility is to respect and honor her husband as head. Then hopefully he will assume his role and gain confidence. She says nothing, but obediently accepts his decisions whether they are wise or not, whether they hurt the family or not, because he, not the wife, will answer the Judge in the end.

This arrangement is certainly a sad waste of the wife's personal strengths and abilities. Like the too-taut tent, it completely ignores her intelligence and insight.

This tent will likely collapse, if indeed it ever gets up. In the meantime, the occupants suffer from a lack of care and direction.

FAIRLY SECURE

This next tent is put up corporately by husband and wife. Although the wife sees how the tent raising can be accomplished, she expects and allows her husband to exert his strength and direct the process. But he also accepts her suggestions and assistance.

Periodically, they disagree and criticize each other; they may argue about who's working the hardest. Because they both need praise and appreciation, friction and competition may develop between them as they struggle with ways and means.

This tent goes up quickly and looks pretty secure from the outside, but there's quite a bit of restlessness and misunderstanding inside.

COLLAPSED

All around we see collapsed tents, evidence that those in charge either couldn't work together, got discouraged, didn't follow instructions or had too much outside interference. Someone carelessly knocked down the center poles after they were up. The former occupants of these tents became fed up with tenting and are now separated, hurt and lonely.

Did you recognize your tent?

2
THE VIEW FROM INSIDE THE TENT

COUNSELORS agree that it's mostly wives who seek help. Women seem to spot troubles in the tent first and are more often concerned about the techniques and swiftness of tent raising. While willingly accepting personal blame, they openly express dissatisfaction with the man in charge.

Listen to snatches of actual conversation held with wives from the various tents —

FROM A SAGGY AND LOOSE TENT

"Husbands are to lead the home. Right? That's what the Bible says," Janeen declared. "But Bob really seems to resist the whole idea. His mother ran her home, so he expects me to run ours. I wish he wouldn't leave it all to me though, 'cause I'm tired of making the decisions."

"Frank has great interest in making decisions regarding building a patio or making investments in the stock market," Ann complained. "But let a household decision or discipline problem come up, and he dismisses it with 'Whatever you do is O.K. with me.' I want him to be in charge."

Janeen and Ann both know that their husbands should and could lead. But because they do not, their marriages resemble saggy and loose tents. They need help in understanding their husbands and knowing how to involve them in home management.

FROM A SLANTED AND LOPSIDED TENT

"What bugs me," Beverly confided, "is that Robby talks a blue streak to others. But when we two are alone or just driving somewhere, it's complete silence unless I start a conversation. We used to talk a lot before we got married."

"Why is it," Janie questioned, "that the kids can tear the place apart and John just walks away, leaving me with all the disciplining? He acts like the kids and house are my total responsibility."

"Things completely fall apart when I'm gone. I have to work full-time to help pay bills and I feel he should share the work load around the house. He doesn't seem to know how to handle anything except his job."

Because it requires understanding and communication to get a husband to talk and to help his wife, a lopsided tent will never stand straight until the wife uses her ability to draw him out and encourage him to act.

FROM A TOO-TAUT TENT

"Clyde thinks I'm going overboard with expressing myself," Evelyn commented. "He's been calling me a 'libber' and says he liked me better when I had no opinions. But I'm really convinced my ideas aren't so bad after all."

"Whatever happens," Gloria lamented, "it's always my fault. Just once I'd like to hear Steve say, 'I was wrong' or 'You are right!'"

The arrogant and unyielding husband pitches a tent that's so tight, it's bound to rip. Some of these husbands are actually afraid the woman will take over and browbeat them. They feel they have to keep the woman in her place.

This type of husband needs to learn how to appreciate and listen to his wife and help her to find personal worth. In doing this, he will realize his own personal worth.

FROM A WOBBLY CENTER POLE TENT

"Gambling gets Pete's check," Tina shared. "The kids do need shoes and I desperately need dental work done, but he's in charge. Some time he'll have to realize that his poor money management is ruining us.

"He's a great guy in other ways. But in the winter, he doesn't have steady work, and it's not my place to tell him what to do. I just pray for good weather and stretch the food budget."

Although this wife is willing to be submissive, putting her head in the sand will not help her marriage grow strong. It's ideal for a husband to work and manage his family's affairs, but when he lacks discipline and maturity, the tent threatens to collapse unless the wife steps in with a little bit of leadership. This wife needs enlightenment about her God-given abilities.

FROM A FAIRLY SECURE TENT

"My problem may seem stupid to you," Betty said quietly, "but I've got to tell someone. Jack works hard, keeps the yard nice and we agree on most everything, but he seldom tells me he loves me. Some days he ignores me entirely until bedtime. Is that normal? He doesn't mistreat me, don't get me wrong. I just want to be appreciated as a person, not just as an object."

"After football, I'm Number One on Adam's list," Alice sighed. "He's the nicest guy in the world but aren't his priorities wrong? Why, I can't get him to go anywhere anymore because of television sports—and nowadays they seem to be year-round specials. I'm only allowed to talk during commercials."

These tenters are suffering needlessly from little rips. Their tents would be much more secure if they knew that a marriage relationship needs to grow. With a little help, they could learn to express their needs and the importance of trying to fulfill their mate's desires.

FROM A COLLAPSING TENT

"Dave's mother has a hold on him which I can't loosen," Helen shared. "He spends more time with her than with me. I keep up with him through her. I feel more like a sister than a wife."

"I miss going to church and I believe our children should be in Sunday school," Karen said. "But Jim has no church background and says he doesn't need God for himself. He doesn't stand in my way, but I don't want to go alone. I feel it's just as much his responsibility to set the example."

Unless their husbands share equal interest and responsibility in pitching their tents, Helen and Karen are fighting a losing battle. Family interference and conflicting value systems wreck many marriages. Even though these marriages began for the wrong reasons, with more concentrated help, some of these relationships can be salvaged.

These interviews — quoting only the wives — may sound one-sided. But they do voice a common complaint among wives. And though sometimes we hate to acknowledge them, these problems and more do exist at one time or another to varying degrees in nearly all marriages.

I'm quite aware that husbands have plenty to complain about too. And when we hear from them later on, you'll see that many husbands are just as willing as their wives to accept help and share the load in correcting attitudes and actions. They also want strong and sturdy tents.

Remember though, that — as a rule — men keep things to themselves until the problems enter the very serious stage when it is often too late to act. So very often, through her special gift of encouragement, the first move is up to the wife when it comes to pitching, propping or putting a tent in order.

3
THE TENTERS' DILEMMA

Why in some marriages is the man in charge seemingly so weak? Why is he unable or unwilling to take the lead in a marriage?

THE TENTERS' IDEAL

The Bible in Ephesians 5:22-25 speaks clearly about the man's lofty position as head of the wife.

Wives, submit yourselves unto your own husbands, as unto the Lord.

For the husband is the head of the wife, even as Christ is the head of the church; and he is the saviour of the body.

Therefore as the church is subject unto Christ, so let the wives be to their own husbands in every thing.

Husbands, love your wives, even as Christ also loved the church, and gave himself for it.

There are not many homes where this spiritual attitude prevails — not even in the homes of Christian professionals. Mary speaks for many wives when she says, "If my husband would love me like Christ loved the Church, I could submit."

Husbands counter with "According to the Scripture, the wife is to submit herself first. When she does this, I'll be able to love her like God commanded and assume leadership of the home."

The result of this rigidity is a stalemate. Then later, if battles are settled without Christian love, the strain of the one's loss and the other's win prevails.

Establishing the ideal relationship is neither quick nor easy. Placing a wedding band on the third finger of his bride's left hand does not suddenly transform an inexperienced groom into a mature husband who loves his wife perfectly and who is able at once to lead a home expertly in every complex area of economic, social and spiritual responsibility. Nor does receiving that ring on her finger guarantee that the young bride can instantly reverence her husband or be in immediate and total submission to him.

If the marriage is dynamic, not static, achieving the ideal relationship is possible. But it takes time. And it takes growth — growth on the part of both partners.

Such growth is not only possible but necessary. David and Vera Mace, well-known Quaker counselors in marriage enrichment, affirm that marriages can and must grow, lest they die.

That growth will occur if each partner views problems as obstacles. A problem suggests something that stops progress, whereas an obstacle carries with it the possibility and probability of surmounting. Admittedly, overcoming obstacles is a struggle. But the Maces' suggested strategy lies in our being committed to handling struggles. With God's help, that is.

AN AFFIRMATIVE DEFINITION

Scores of Christian couples believe that living in a tight tent will surely bring them happiness. They substitute a standard of living or a set of rigid rules in place of loving and working towards relationships and understanding each other. They assume that, as Christians, they are completed products.

Then when things go wrong — and they invariably do — such couples try to keep it a secret from observers, because preserving the appearance of the tent seems to be more important than mending the little rips. They don't seem to realize that a bad situation doesn't automatically improve or go away just because years pile up.

Eliminate the Negative

What does submission mean? That the wife has no right to opinions or feelings? That she has to be happy inside the tent all the time, whether she likes it or not? That she is personal servant to the husband's least desires?

Is submission of the woman just for the man's

convenience and pleasure? Just to keep her in control? Should she become weak and insignificant to make him appear stronger? Should she lock her mind away? Does it mean that the wife is not spiritually free to follow the Lord?

No, submission does not. Submission and subservience are not the same. All these ideas imply subservience, a relationship of involuntary servitude for the partner who is forced or obligated to relinquish control and give the other partner the upper hand.

Charlie Shedd writes to his daughter in *Letters to Karen*, "I see some men who never get the message. They operate under the delusion that a successful husband is one who imprisons 'the little woman' within the prison of his desires.

"Some women give in to this treatment and resign their individuality. But this is not living, and it is never marriage at its best."[1]

Accentuate the Positive

Biblical submission is a positive concept, a relationship in which one partner willingly allows the other to be in command. You see, submission is only submission when there's a willing heart behind it. According to Scripture, the wife is to submit herself!

Charlie Shedd put it beautifully in his *Letters to Philip:* "Man as head is not that of a mighty potentate sitting on his throne, ruling his cowering subjects with an iron hand. This is more like a conductor standing on his box directing a symphony. Delicate, but definite! Subdued, yet powerful!...It seems to me that nearly every woman I know wants a man who knows how to love, with authority."[2]

I am submissive to Jim in areas where I am comfortable with his ability to lead. He acknowledges areas where I am particularly gifted—like disciplining the children. I want him to be in charge. I don't like to bear that weight. Yet, he loves me too much to take unfair advantage of me and use his position for selfish desires. I love him too much to rob him of his protective and authoritative position.

Jim wants to help me reach my potential of personal worth just as I want to help him. We're constantly adjusting to each other's growth and needs.

Our personal goals—if they are God's goals—will never conflict, for neither of us will *knowingly* step on the other in order to reach a personal goal. Keeping communication free and open with one another about our feelings and opinions lies at the heart of our contentment.

Remember, a tent is only a tool, a shelter and protection to enable the campers inside to enjoy the camping experience mutually. The late Peter Marshall said, "Marriage is not a federation of two sovereign states. It is a union—domestic, social, spiritual, physical. It is a fusion of two hearts—the union of two lives—the coming together of two tributaries, which, after being joined in marriage, will flow in the same channel in the same direction...carrying the same burdens of responsibility and obligation."[3]

Therefore, I see the unselfish attitudes toward

submission and perfect Christ-like love, not as the starting position in marriage, but as goals towards which both husbands and wives work.

As Howard Hendricks puts it, "Submission is not the exclusive responsibility of the woman. Submission is the life-style of the Christian."[4]

A WIFE'S PERSPECTIVE

Let's face it, some men don't take the lead in the home because they honestly don't know how to lead. How many men have actually had the privilege of observing their own fathers confidently lead at home? Home management is a tremendous task and responsibility to tackle without any orientation or training.

Generally speaking, men are afraid to try something new if they might fail. Because their women find it natural and easy to take over a situation, some men are afraid even to try. And men seem to get discouraged more easily than women. Most of the men I interviewed bore this fact out.

One man after learning that as a husband he was to assume full authority and leadership in financial, spiritual and disciplinary matters said, "Ruth, I feel like running away."

Jim and I have noticed in our counseling that men seem to be more private about their faith than women. This is a real bone of contention to some wives who desperately want their husbands to lead spiritually. A few husbands do lead. But even some pastors and missionaries, committed to God's work, are a bit timid about leading their own families in worship.

In our own home, since I felt the burden for family worship and had access to and time with the children when they were young, I led out. Jim was for it but needed action — encouragement.[5]

Don't Throw Any Boomerangs

Instead of giving encouragement, however, many domineering wives treat their husbands

with great disrespect, abusing them with criticism and sarcasm as though they owned their spouses and had a right to humiliate and hurt them. But when a wife puts her husband down, she is really injuring herself. Many wives are unaware of this boomerang factor in marriage.

Do Prime the Pump

Most men need the stimulus of female ideas and verbal encouragement, just like some manual water pumps need a bit of priming to get them started. This priming may be a bit of encouragement and expertise that the wife has the natural

ability to give. When the husband takes hold, she can let up. Some men already possess this self-starting action, so the wife need only appreciate and encourage it.

A study of the foreign mission field reveals situations where women saw and answered a desperate need to share the gospel even though there were few men to direct and shoulder the heavy responsibility. Like Mary Slessor of Calibar, Amy Carmichael and Mother Theresa, to name a few.

Then gradually, men caught their vision and began to share the load. New missionary work is now more widespread and complex because men have added their strength and ingenuity to the impetus of the women.

A HUSBAND'S DILEMMA

I asked men what part their wives played in the leadership of the home and how they felt about it. Here are some excerpts from those conversations.

A Personal Puppet

"My wife is so eager for me to lead that she will nag me to death (a type of leading) until I do it. Then she'll stand back and tell me what I did or said that was wrong. She's still telling me what to do. Sometimes, I feel like her private puppet."

Some wives tell their husbands when to lead and what to say, then try to convince friends — and themselves — that their husbands are in charge.

A Perfectionist's Mate

"Angie tries too hard to be perfect. That makes me nervous because I'm not perfect and I don't expect her to be. I just want her to be relaxed and do the best she can. I have accepted her just like she is with her strengths and weaknesses, and I don't expect her to measure up to all the standards professionals speak and write about. She's always wanting to analyze and change our system."

Don't take everything the professionals write as Holy Writ. Remember, many experts are simply little spurts away from home. Even if women read all the professional advice books on the market today with their many fad formulas for happy marriages, the only thing they could be certain of would be their own uncertainty.

A Glorified Father

Ron prefers that his wife assume responsibility at home. "I want to provide money and support, but I expect her to make all the home decisions. I'll make all the big decisions; she can make the little ones."

He feels a wife and mother should take care of these routine matters, yet he has another complaint.

"She's like a little girl," he said. "She constantly calls me at work to ask me insignificant things. She really has better ideas than I do, because I haven't been home all day with the kids and I really don't know what's best for them at that particular time. I want her to be the mother. It's a hassle."

Women's minds are detailed for the purpose of supplementing the man's ideas, not just for handling the little things.

An Intimidating Husband

This husband fears that he overwhelms his wife. "My wife, Jeanie, is better disciplined than I am. She can look way ahead and see problems coming. I appreciate her suggestions. But she constantly puts herself down and because she is afraid of making the wrong decision, she won't make any. I get madder at her for that than for her actually going ahead and making a wrong decision. So what if she flubs up once in a while? She's human.

"She just kind of folds up when I come on the scene. I don't know why I intimidate her. I just want to support her decisions."

Paul Tournier, the Swiss physician and theologian says, "Indecision is a poison as far as the person is concerned. It always arises from some inner conflict which one has not had the courage to resolve, or even to become aware of. It is common among those who have been kept in a state of dependence by domineering parents. It can persist through life long after the death of the parents. Such people will tell us quite openly that they do not even know what their tastes, their beliefs and their aims in life are. As soon as they have made a decision they begin wondering if they have not made a mistake."[6]

In this case, the husband will need to encourage the wife by acknowledging her good decisions and by gently persuading her to accept more responsibility. Eventually, she'll be able to give him the type of encouragement he needs.

An Object of Criticism

Men resent it when women become know-it-alls. They resent it so much that they will shut out all suggestions and keep their ideas and dreams — the very fabric from which a marriage is made — to themselves.

Anita is an example. She says, "O.K. Do it your own way, but it's not going to work. We'll just see what happens. Remember the deal last month? We're still paying for it!"

"She second-guesses me every time," Barry groaned. "If it turns out that she was right, she blasts out with 'I told you so.' "

Is it any wonder Barry keeps his ideas to himself?

Anita has stopped being a partner and become a foe. She needs to hold the flashlight, at least, while her husband steadies the tent. A wife, after listening to her husband's plans, making observations and asking questions, is wise to support him. And she should be prepared to bear and share the consequences with him, whatever they are, without recriminations.

A WOMAN'S INFLUENCE

It's been well said that a woman can make or break a man. The devil was wise. The surest way to Adam was through Eve. Genesis 3:6 records: *She took of the fruit thereof, and did eat, and gave also unto her husband with her; and he did eat.*

Remember, too, it was Rebecca, Isaac's wife, who conceived the idea of their son Jacob deceiving his father. And Samson was ruined because Delilah, taking advantage of his weakness, discovered the source of his strength and used it against him.

Solomon's spiritual and political downfall emanated from his idol-worshiping wives. We could name many men whose failures point to a woman's conniving, criticism, greed or lack of support. But there are just as many whose great successes hinge on appreciative and loving wives who stood behind them with encouragement and confidence. It's no secret that Martin Luther, Dwight L. Moody, Winston Churchill, Harry S Truman and many more leaned heavily on their wives. Singer Johnny Cash openly credits his wife June Carter Cash for his success.

Women may be weaker physically, but it's a marvel to see a robust, prominent man controlled and helped by a slip of a woman. Such a situation may be good or bad, but it's a fact of life.

Speaking in generalities again, women are quick thinkers and great persuaders. They're in a hurry to get that tent up, too. They flare up in anger quickly but get discouraged less easily, whereas men tend to be more contemplative, slower to get angry, but more troubled by discouragement. Not true in every case, but a lot of the time.

A WIFE'S GIFT

Because men think in blocks, they are equipped to tackle big things and bear very heavy loads of responsibility in the home, community and world. They have the vision and creativity to build skyscrapers and design networks of roads. They also have the capability of giving the woman the protection she loves and needs.

Women, on the other hand, tend to be apprehensive about big decisions like long-term commitments or a heavy debt. So men depend on the wives' cautious, detailed little steps which serve as a governor to their daring and impulsive natures. A husband's decisions are better when influenced by the wife's suggestions.

God has given women unusual skill in the art of persuasion, and the ability to encourage men to tackle and complete jobs they thought they couldn't do. So a wife's greatest strength and most significant contribution in a marriage partnership lies in encouraging her husband to do those big things he or she could never accomplish alone.

Men need to hear things like:

"I believe in you."

"I trust your judgment."

"I'm proud of you."

"I'm behind you."

"I'm glad you're home."

It's evident that this selfless attitude doesn't just happen. We need to learn how to incorporate it into our minds and hearts and then communicate it.

This will not only get the tent up quickly and properly, but will pave the way for solving big and little problems and dealing with tensions as they arise, like contending with wet wood midst a week of rain at our campsite.

The key to this attitude is found in Ephesians 5:20-21: *Giving thanks always for all things unto God and the Father in the name of our Lord Jesus Christ;*

Submitting yourselves one to another in the fear of God.

Ironically, this passage comes before the instructions to husbands that they love their wives as Christ loved the Church, and to wives that they be in submission to their husbands.

THE IDEAL RELATIONSHIP

Mutual submission is the basis of Christian brotherly love which is also mentioned in Romans 12:10. *Be kindly affectioned one to another with brotherly love; in honour preferring one another.*

Husbands and wives are bound to love each other in this way, by submitting one to another. Unless this first step in brotherly love is taken, the second step toward perfect love will never be realized.

In the first years of marriage, a man can no more love his wife perfectly as Christ loved the Church, or the woman be in total submission, than a marathon runner can become a gold medalist at the Olympics after the first bout of training. A husband's love will mature as the wife encourages him by stabilizing the center pole of the tent or holding up the sides, whatever help he needs. Her submission will develop naturally.

When we analyze how Christ loved the Church, we find that He accepted believers (the Church) as they were with all their imperfections. He loved the Church for what it would become. Jesus named

31

Peter the "Rock" long before his great declaration of faith (see Matthew 16:18 and Acts 2:14-36), Jesus knew what Peter would become.

Heritage and environment affect every individual, creating weak and strong points in his or her personality. Therefore, two imperfect people are going to constitute imperfections when they form a marriage union.

As Cecil Osborne describes this, "The gospel does not condemn us for the weakness and failures resulting from a faulty environment. We are not held responsible for that. We are held responsible only for what we do with our marred, faulty lives from here on out, considering the damaged persons we all are. Christ's cry from the cross, 'Father forgive them; for they know not what they do' (Luke 23:34, *RSV*), carries with it the implication that their personalities and reactions were formed by a thousand factors. Only God could assess the blame or fix responsibility."[7]

Our big job then is to get acquainted with our own basic strengths and weaknesses and those of our spouse: to understand why we have certain major and minor problems. Then we can learn how to adjust and compromise in order to create one strong personality.

In his book, *Between Parent and Teenager*, Haim Ginott stresses that, at first, a lover sees only the strengths in the beloved. But as the love relationship matures, the lover accepts the strengths while also acknowledging the weaknesses.

Until couples learn to appreciate and love each other as Christian brothers and sisters and to communicate on that basis, the satisfying and comfortable position of husband as head and wife in submission will never be realized. Submission of the wife cannot be imposed any more than loving as Christ loved can be demanded.

Ephesians 4:1-3 gives this helpful advice: *Walk worthy of the vocation wherewith ye are called, with all lowliness and meekness, with longsuffering, forbearing one another in love: Endeavouring to keep the unity of the Spirit in the bond of peace.*

This is real unity and the only sure way to put up a strong tent which will weather any storm or calamity.

Footnotes

1. Charlie W. Shedd, *Letters to Karen: On Keeping Love in Marriage* (Nashville, Tennessee: Abingdon Press, 1965), p. 30.

2. Charlie W. Shedd, *Letters to Philip: On How to Treat a Woman* (New York: Doubleday & Co., 1968), p. 13.

3. Catherine Marshall, *A Man Called Peter* (New York: Harper and Row, 1957), p. 201.

4. Howard G. Hendricks, *Heaven Help the Home!* (Wheaton, Illinois: Victor Books, 1974), p. 31.

5. My book, *Devotions, a Family Affair* (Master's Press, Kalamazoo, Michigan, 1977), carries a more detailed account of our personal growth in this area.

6. Paul Tournier, *The Meaning of Persons* (New York: Harper and Row, 1957), p. 201.

7. Cecil B. Osborne, *The Art of Learning to Love Yourself* (Grand Rapids, Michigan: Zondervan Corporation, 1976), p. 33.

4

THE CAMPER'S CHALLENGE

Inexperienced campers often discover to their dismay that the quality of the tent they chose is inadequate for the season's needs. Not only do some brands not include enough strong rope for guy lines, but they also lack extra-sturdy stakes for rocky ground.

In their rush to get started, novice campers don't realize that they will also need a hammer or hatchet, lantern and shovel. So progress is often extremely slow and full of disappointment and frustration.

Pressures to set up quickly may also result in a poor choice of campsite. During a rainy night many campers woefully realize that their tent was pitched in a gully. Pity the poor husband who is forced to defend his intelligence that night!

Inexperience, poor tools and lack of preparation can adversely affect marriage relationships, too.

SOCIAL AND EMOTIONAL PRESSURES

Phyllis and Chip are very young and have been married only a few months. Both worked at the same place before marriage and one of them was required to quit. Phyllis did. Chip comes home tired after facing people all day. Phyllis wants to talk. He's not very congenial and when she confronts him about it, he accuses her of wanting her job back. Then he sulks.

Chip's divorced mother, who leans on him, adds extra strain on them financially and emotionally. When Phyllis challenges Chip about his mother, he counters with digs about her meals and house cleaning — always inadequate for the day. She feels like leaving and says so. This infuriates Chip and makes him very defensive and bitter.

Right now, Chip and Phyllis are both very insecure and immature. Since their trust is so young and fragile, their marriage could easily break apart under the strain.

Other couples seeking answers to their difficulties gain perspective when they analyze the poor and shallow bases for their marriages. People marry for many reasons —

- a desire to leave home
- pregnancy
- the need for security
- a desire for companionship
- the fear of single living
- a feeling of sympathy
- the search for happiness.

Christians and non-Christians alike marry for these reasons. Yet marriages built on these grounds — most often those involving teenagers who lack the maturity and stamina to correct and build on mistakes — rarely work, unless someone experienced offers steady help and guidance.

INADEQUATE OR CARELESS PLANS

In their excitement and elation about going camping, casual campers who do little planning also run into snags, because they neglect the proper tools. Finding a rock to pound in stakes is trying and frustrating, no matter what quality tent a person has to put up. Using a hammer or hatchet would be so much easier than wielding a rock. Bad weather will also magnify inadequate preparation or tools.

So marriages, though based on real love rather than infatuation and emotional circumstances, are also likely to develop serious problems after the honeymoon stage is over. That's when unresolved differences surface. These differences may include —
- unequal or interfaith beliefs
- mismatched goals
- different value systems
- cultural differences
- parental interference
- poor communication
- financial instability.

These marriages, too, often end in divorce. But frequently, mates just learn to endure the differences and mismatching — especially after children come along — resigning themselves to a living divorce. Each goes his own way and has his or her own set of friends — partners merely sharing home and finance and children.

Christians often find themselves part of these problem marriages. Churches tried to ignore the problems for a while, but more recently real help is being extended to these victims of poor choice.

It's tough, but possible to work through the snarls by relying on one's personal faith and developing a positive attitude of appreciation for cultural differences and personality traits, along with capitalizing on the wife's special gift of encouragement.

These tents can be mended and strengthened and eventually provide protection, happiness and safety for the occupants. It will take a long time for some husbands to reach the goal of loving their wives as Christ loved the Church. And the submission of wives to their husbands doesn't come instantly. But it's certainly better to attempt to mend a marriage than to discard it without trying.

ADJUSTMENTS AND COMPROMISE

Even well-matched campers who are prepared and organized still run into difficulties when they enter unfamiliar territory.

It would be wonderful, though not possible, to anticipate all the obstacles that will surface in a partnership. After all, marriage is a series of little and big crises which reveal insecurities, cultural differences and disagreements. Each difficulty requires immediate compromise and eventual adjustment.

These partnerships rarely dissolve unless one

party refuses to cooperate and carry his or her share of the load. The wife is usually more sensitive about areas of weakness. If she is willing to adjust and compromise, her husband usually will too.

Lance Webb advises, "Accept the things you cannot change. Quit fighting the facts of your situation. This may mean accepting many minor or even major faults in those with whom you live which you would like to change, but which when attacked simply cause you and them to lose other things far more precious. Change the things that you can change. Work with others on their level, not against them from a higher level. Your symptoms of sin may be different from theirs but your sin is the same; prideful self-love seeking to save your false-image."[1]

When husbands and wives both recognize that the need for regular mending and reinforcing along the way is normal, they will relax and be able to take their potentially good marriage and confidently move forward toward forming an ideal union.

Footnote

1. Lance Webb, *Discovering Love* (Nashville, Tennessee: Abingdon Press, 1946), p. 144.

5
MENDING THE TENT

Appreciating the leadership ability and encouragement needs of a man, and understanding the supporting strength of a woman merely set the stage for building a strong and meaningful relationship.

It is not an easy matter to pool likes and dislikes, differentiate convictions from whims, separate securities from insecurities and distinguish between wants and needs. A couple does well to recognize the underlying factors on which every marriage is built. Then partners can anticipate the tensions that develop while staying abreast of them.

The old adage, "a stitch in time saves nine" — getting a little help before a tiny tear becomes a jagged rip — applies here. Knowing this, good campers will wisely, and without apology, strengthen and mend their tents in the process of pitching them.

These are the areas around which marriages revolve —
- faith
- goals
- finance
- children
- in-laws
- communication
- appreciation
- sexual relationships.

FAITH THAT MATCHES

It's unbelievable how many engaged couples discuss every part of marriage except the spiritual aspect. They may have significant differences in denominations or religions, but seem confident that these things can be worked out after marriage. But solutions are really tough to arrive at after marriage.

Considering the Spiritual

Not talking about these important spiritual aspects is like putting up a tent without any thought of projected wants and needs — an inadequate and cramped situation. It's possible for two people to be compatible without spiritual oneness, but this is not an ideal arrangement since a good spiritual understanding affects other problem solving. Spiritual oneness is so important in a marriage that to avoid the subject is like cutting a huge chunk out of a relationship.

People hold dearly to what they learned or did as children. When that is threatened, they become insecure and defensive. Often explosive.

Why?

Because what we are as individuals is so entwined with what we believe or don't believe about God that to alter our beliefs or change our worship patterns drastically introduces many frictions into a relationship. "We always did it this way" or "our minister said ..." usually introduces the touchy subjects that many people are unsure about anyway.

Accepting the Lord

If your spouse has never accepted the Lord, invite him/her to do so. It's a shame how many people selfishly withhold their personal faith. It's amazing, also, how many mates feel threatened when their partners have a Christ loyalty. They resent the time and money given to church activities. Often the one with faith feels stifled because the spiritual dimension to his life is not being satisfied.

A good example is Julie and John who came for premarital counseling. John is a Christian. We chatted easily about their plans, jobs, friends, finances, etc. When I asked about spiritual things, there was silence.

'What is your relationship with the Lord?" I asked Julie. (I knew about John's.)

"What do you mean?" she asked. "I'm a member

of a church and I pray sometimes. Especially when I'm upset," she added quickly, "if that's what you mean?"

"Have you ever heard about accepting Christ personally?"

"No, I don't think so."

"You didn't know that John had accepted the Lord?"

"No, he never told me about it," she said, throwing an inquisitive look his way.

"No, I've never told her," John admitted solemnly, "because I'm not walking as close to the Lord as I know I should. Or as I once did. But I've wanted to many times."

"Maybe you'd like to tell her right now, John," I prompted. "She deserves to know about it."

With confidence, he shared his testimony about when he met Christ. His eyes sparkled and Julie listened spellbound.

I admit this put John on the spot, but it was good for him too. It was all the encouragement he needed. And it was the beginning of a beautiful discussion about the importance of inviting Jesus into a life and a marriage.

As a couple gets older and the family comes along, spiritual matters become more important. It's a tremendous sacrifice to have pledged yourself to someone who does not share personal faith in Christ or rely on His provisions. Spiritual value systems must be balanced for a marriage to be completely satisfying.

Peter Marshall says that the "marriage relationship is the most delightful and sacred of human relations. It is the clasping of hands, the blending of lives and union of hearts, that two may walk together up the hill of life to meet the dawn — together bearing life's burdens, discharging its duties...sharing its joys and sorrows."[1]

Without Christ as the center such a relationship as Marshall describes is impossible. That's why Paul offers this excellent advice in 2 Corinthians 6:14: *Be ye not unequally yoked together with unbelievers: for what fellowship hath righteousness with unrighteousness? and what communion hath light with darkness?*

For a Christian to marry an unbeliever, then, is to take an unwarranted risk. Inevitably, the Christian partner can expect unhappiness, conflicting values, lack of communication and distress.

Nevertheless, if you're already in that dilemma, the Lord can and will help you. In fact, He's the only solution to a problem like that. Many adjustments in marriage are bigger than a couple can handle alone, so a joint faith in Christ is essential.

Choosing a Church

When spouses have different denominational backgrounds, even when both partners know the Lord personally, there are bound to be painful compromises and adjustments. Small differences in past experience between formal or informal worship can lead to heated debate.

When we were married, I changed to Jim's denomination. Even though our beliefs were identical, just learning a new system of church government and mission outreach, along with a less formal mode of worship, required a lot of adjust-

45

ment for me. At the same time, Jim has been very careful to appreciate my former denomination and my home church family because I spent my formative years there and am greatly indebted to those wonderful people who loved me and led me in my relationship to Jesus.

A couple recently shared with us that each set of parents bugged them so about which church they'd attend, that they felt hypocritical in even going to church at all. Finally they made their own choice of church. Now they serve and worship not to appease their parents, but as an expression of their own faith.

I really ache for those couples who share their life together in other respects, but who are separated in church relationships. Going to separate churches is not a satisfactory solution for any husband and wife, because that postpones a decision as parents about where the children will attend. Too often, couples from different church backgrounds compromise by not going to church at all.

One of the best securities in a marriage is the friends a couple makes. Unless they share the same church, they risk not having the same friends — friends who will bolster their faith. We are greatly influenced by our peers. Each couple needs friends outside of the family for encouragement.

So it's better to have all the heated discussion about religion and church before marriage. For if you disagree before marriage, you will certainly disagree after marriage. And arguments after marriage take on a different hue. Women seem to find it easier to talk about spiritual matters, so the

dialogue will probably depend on their encouragement and courage.

GOALS THAT CHALLENGE

Next to faith, goals head the list in importance
because they become factors either of friction or
future fulfillment. A marriage needs two kinds of
goals, far-reaching and short-term, to insure
growth. It's like a tent needing both stakes and
guy lines for stability.

"Talk to an average couple about marital growth
and their minds go blank," say David and Vera
Mace. "You are virtually the same person the day
after your wedding as you were the day before.
Changes will indeed come.... If you don't act to
'take hold' of the relationship, it will, like a rud-
derless ship, simply drift wherever the currents
carry it."[2]

Jim's and my far-reaching goal at marriage was
to lead a congregation. Before that goal could be
reached, however, we needed to set some short
term goals of training and maturity. There was
much schooling involved, as well as establishing a
close walk with the Lord ourselves.

Unless goals coincide, problems erupt. If one
partner's goal is luxurious living or spending all
on self, and the other prefers to live just comfort-
ably and use excess money to help others and support the Lord's work, conflict will be sharp. The
wife can't very well encourage her husband if their
goals are different.

Researching your various goals is excellent preparation. Consulting an insurance expert or attor-

47

ney, reading books and articles on the subject will aid a couple in the wise use of time and money.

FINANCES THAT STRETCH

No matter what the far-reaching goals are, finances are an automatic concern for each couple. For statistics prove that finances cause more problems in marriage than any other factor. In his book, *Heaven Help the Home!* Howard Hendricks states that 50% of marital problems involve finances.

So not looking ahead to money needs is like failing to dig a water trench around your tent. Even the best-looking tents get flooded by mistake.

Before Jim and I got married, we visited with my boss, the Executive Director of the American Oil and Chemical Company. She advised us that not more than one-third of a person's earnings should go for housing. We've followed that advice fairly closely and found it to be accurate.

Establishing Credit

My boss also warned us against credit buying. We appreciate her counsel even more today than we did before we got married. For credit buying carries with it a real risk when used irresponsibly.

Before you can cash a check or prove identity these days, it is almost a necessity to establish credit. But the ease of obtaining credit and the hard-sell pressures of advertising dupe young couples into overextending themselves right into bankruptcy. We hear about such cases daily.

When one mate has little buying resistance, carrying credit cards becomes a dangerous sport. Before buying bargains on credit, couples need to calculate carefully the interest they pay on such credit card purchases. I myself have been guilty of saving so much on bargains that I put our family finances in terrible straits.

Talking About Money

If one mate makes all the money decisions, that mate will in essence control the home. Yet whether the wife contributes to the income or not, the money acquired belongs to both partners. So both partners need to talk about it.

Jim and I have probably had more discussions about finances than about any other matter. So we've learned from scratch how to talk about money.

Earmark a regular time to discuss finances when both are rested, rather than when a discrepancy or an overdrawn notice from the bank forces the issue. And take my word for it, the worst times to discuss money mix-ups are before retiring or at mealtime.

As Charlie Shedd puts it, "Every husband-wife combination brings to the marriage different concepts. One may have been brought up by parents who indulged every want. The other may be tied up inside with a poverty complex. This person might have been raised on the installment plan. Perhaps the other heard over and over 'strictly cash! save first, then buy!' There are dozens of other differences out of your backgrounds that may need to analyzed."[3]

So talk it all out. Remember, talking about money matters is like keeping the tent trench free of debris. It's the only way to keep water out of the tent and to avoid a messy, muddy area around the entrance. This means that occasionally the campers have to buck the storm to clear things out of the trench. Like clearing trenches, talking about money is not always pleasant, but certainly necessary.

Using a Budget

Family finances certainly deserve some sort of plan — a budget. A budget is a guide used to anticipate and allow for regular expenditures, thus curbing impulsive and unnecessary buying (I don't know where I picked up that statement, but it's been in my head for years!).

Perhaps neither partner has had any prior exposure to budget living. Be that as it may, it takes only one thoroughly flooded tent to prove the value of digging a deep, protective trench before settling in. Prevent such disasters in your tent by a little cautious pre-planning and wise budgeting.

There are many types of budgets to consider. The local library is one good source of information on budgeting for your family requirements. Other possible sources for budget ideas are older friends, your parents, his parents, your pastor or perhaps an accountant. In some areas, budget counselors are also available to assist.

Whatever the source of your ideas, choose the budget that best suits your family. Some people have a very simple budget like Charlie Shedd who says they give 10%, save 10% and spend the rest with thanksgiving and praise.

When Jim and I were in college and seminary our budget was so slim we didn't have to write much down. We just watched every penny. My boss had advised us to set up a budget, but we didn't do so until we became overdrawn and had some bitter disagreements about what we should pay and who had bought what.

So we tried the envelope system. After calculating our tithe, rent, utilities, tuition, books, food, doctor, gasoline — things that had to be paid — we set aside for those items first, putting so much a week into each envelope. What was left over we spent for "luxuries" like clothing, stamps and ice cream. Many times we spent our last quarter on two ice cream cones. We always agreed on that.

As our income gradually increased, we added a little insurance. We bought a sewing machine on credit — our first such item. We figured the machine was an investment and we figured right. Our family increased quickly, too, so our reckless buying was held at a bare minimum — usually those ice cream cones.

Christ warned, *For where your heart is, there will your treasure be also* (Luke 12:34). Howard Hendricks advises, therefore, that budgets should flow from family prayer, family planning and periodic evaluation.

Keeping Accounts

Hopefully, a couple is working from a budget, but even when they are not, they still need to keep financial records. And the one who has the most time or enjoys doing accounts the most should be in charge of the books. If this happens to be the husband, the wife with her mind for details can be of valuable help and encouragement to him in balancing the books and choosing priorities.

But no matter who keeps the books, all financial matters should remain a joint affair. If one mate becomes a self-appointed watchdog merely to clamp down on the other's spending, the whole relationship soon gets out of kilter. Each mate should accept part of the responsibility of recording checks and curbing unwise or impulsive spending.

I took care of the books when Jim and I were first married because I had the most time. Because of my background, I was the more conservative of the two, and I squeezed those eagles till they squealed (I've changed a lot since then!).

But I didn't like telling Jim what he could or couldn't spend. I felt like an ogre. So we switched our system. Now he handles the books, while I help him. And he tells me whether or not I can purchase a certain item. We've now got a system of keeping accounts that works for us.

Giving to God

Couples do well to decide before marriage how much they'll give to the Lord's work. Jim and I believe that couples who are generous with the Lord and who practice living by faith will experience greater security and happiness in their marriages.

We particularly like 2 Corinthians 9:7,8: *Every man according as he purposeth in his heart, so let him give; not grudgingly, or of necessity: for God loveth a cheerful giver.*

And God is able to make all grace abound toward you; that ye, always having all sufficiency in all things, may abound to every good work.

Jim and I have sought to apply the truth of these verses to our own resources, because we believe God has promised to provide our needs when we obey Him and trust Him. And we've never missed a meal.

Again, as Charlie Shedd advised his son, Philip, "When you see your money as a means of helping others, or for helping God help others, you have: (a) protected yourselves from the miseries of self-ishness; (b) built in a guard against losing your bearings as you prosper; (c) put yourself in a position to experience one of life's greatest thrills — that of knowing many blessings because you are a blessing to many."[4]

Controlling Wants and Needs

Young marrieds need to learn to want only what they can afford. It bears repeating. They should live within their means, however meager.

Struggling together for survival is one of the strongest cords of the marriage bond. Doing without luxuries does not hurt a young couple's relationship if attitudes are right.

A verse that has helped us regarding financial decisions is James 1:5. *If any of you lack wisdom, let him ask of God, that giveth to all men liberally.* This is not a "giving" verse particularly, but it assures us of God's wisdom when we ask for it. Sometimes this wisdom is especially needed when we must make financial decisions.

Saving Systematically

Saving can be a product of insecurity just as spending lavishly is sometimes a product of ignorance. Combine one partner's frugal saving with the other's wild buying in a marriage and watch the fireworks. Compromise is the only solution.

Often insurance policies can double as savings during the first struggling years of marriage. Another way is to build equity in a home. But whatever the means, every couple should try to save systematically.

Keeping Money Private

Jill says, "My husband's mother often asks how much we have in the bank and what bills we have due. Bill tells her just like it's her business to know. She then gives him money to cover some bills. I don't like that. He got so mad at me when I suggested we give the money back. But I don't want her telling us what to buy."

Bill will have to inform his mother that they are doing fine and can manage on their own. If occasionally she wants to give them a little monetary encouragement, that's fine, but their bills and purchases should be a private affair. Otherwise the one who provides the money will certainly want to control the issues.

It's hard to turn down cold cash, but when it allows or encourages a couple to live above their means and causes tension in the marriage, it should be rejected. It's not worth it.

PLANNING FOR A FAMILY

Desires and plans regarding children should be discussed thoroughly before marriage. We've felt

the awful disappointment when one mate learns after marriage that the other doesn't want children. The pain is critical. It happens a lot.

Find out before marriage if there is any medical or emotional reason why either mate cannot or would rather not have children, so that necessary counseling or medical attention can be sought.

An unplanned child who is also an unwanted child presents unprecedented strife in a family. And the child will no doubt have to learn to overcome emotional scars later in his life.

Anticipatory grandparents often pressure their married children into producing grandchildren prematurely. This causes alienation and some guilt if a couple does not comply.

Contrary to what many people believe, having children will not hold a marriage together if it's in trouble. It may keep the family in the same tent, but the problems created are myriad.

Children certainly are a wonderful gift and heritage from the Lord. Caring for, training and loving them is one of the highest and most sobering callings in life. Psalm 127:3-5 (*NASB*) says it beautifully. *Behold, children are a gift of the Lord; the fruit of the womb is a reward. Like arrows in the hand of a warrior, so are the children of one's youth. How blessed is the man whose quiver is full of them; they shall not be ashamed, when they speak with their enemies in the gate.*

Caring for children affects every part of the personality. It has a way of bringing out the best and worst in people. In fact, many marriages don't know what real problems are until children arrive.

Having children can aggravate already existing situations, say, a tight budget or in-law interference. And children bring with them a host of new problems. For instance, disagreement on discipline alone — how, who and when — keeps many homes electrified with tension and controversy.

So parents really get fully acquainted with each other as they learn to share the responsibility of parenting. Among other things, tendencies toward selfishness and self-centeredness are challenged.

But the responsibilities of being parents are equalled also by the joys and surprises that await new fathers and mothers. For raising children unmasks and utilizes the talents and capabilities of each parent and becomes one of the most worthwhile goals two people can share.[5]

IN-LAWS WHO UNDERSTAND

This chapter is long, but we've not only been digging and clearing trenches, we've also been doing some tent mending. And mending sometimes takes longer than making something new.

So while we're digging out those trenches and mending the tent, let's tackle one last subject that must be considered: in-laws.

Genesis 2:24 says, *Therefore shall a man leave his father and his mother, and shall cleave unto his wife: and they shall be one flesh.*

These instructions were the first ones given to Adam, even before there was any mother or father for him to leave. Great wisdom here. And the same sound advice is repeated both in the gospels and in Ephesians 5:31.

Let's face it, many parents do cause friction and ill will in their married children's lives and are the indirect cause of many divorces. This is where carefully diverting the existing trenches away from the entrance of the tent pays off. Otherwise, muddy water will seep inside and cause much damage.

Some parents will even help divert the trenches downhill, forcing their married children to stand on their own feet and face their own problems.

That's also called "cutting the apron strings."

Living with in-laws is to be avoided, unless there is simply no alternative to consider. Wise young couples, except in unusual situations, can say without apology to either set of parents, "We love you too much to live with you or even next door to you." Where parents are possessive as well as close, it is sometimes best for couples to move to another city or state so they can struggle together and have a life of their own.

For some reason, trouble often emanates from the husband's side of the family, usually from his mother — despite the jokes often aimed at the wife's mother. And when eruptions occur on the husband's side of the family, he needs to do the digging out and diverting.

When interferences come from the wife's side of the family, it's her responsibility to be the spokesman. This little formula has eased many, many problems in struggling marriages.

Robert confided that he and Ellen were having problems involving his family. She resented them very much, but there was no way the couple could avoid them. The conflict was constant.

"Then I began to study my wife's parents," Robert said. "And I noticed that her dad always kissed her mother goodbye and hello and gave her special time. I figured that maybe this is what Ellen expected in our marriage, even though my parents didn't act this way.

"So I decided to give it a try. A strange thing happened. I noticed that when I kissed Ellen goodbye and hello and gave her private time, she treated my family a whole lot better."

Robert discovered the secret.

A healthy relationship with parents can be one of the most satisfying dimensions of marriage. Overexposure, however, spoils an otherwise beautiful picture. Careful balance is a necessity.

Now let's tackle the guy lines.

Footnotes

1. Peter Marshall, *John Doe, Disciple: Sermons for the Young* (New York: McGraw-Hill Book Co., 1963), p. 186.
2. David and Vera Mace, *How to Have a Happy Marriage* (Nashville, Tennessee: Abingdon Press, 1977), p. 40.
3. Charlie W. Shedd, *Letters to Philip: On How to Treat a Woman* (New York: Doubleday & Co., 1968), p. 92.
4. Charlie W. Shedd, *Letters to Philip*, p. 95.
5. *How to Really Love Your Child* by Ross Campbell, M.D. (Victor Books) is an excellent guide for parents.

6

ADJUSTING THE GUY LINES

I⊤'s quite an experience to hear wives and husbands exclaim, "I didn't know you felt like that!" or "I had no idea you had that impression."

First Timothy 6:17-19 says: *Charge them that are rich in this world, that they be not highminded, nor trust in uncertain riches, but in the living God, who giveth us richly all things to enjoy;*

That they do good, that they be rich in good works, ready to distribute, willing to communicate.

Arriving at good communication is much like adjusting the guy lines of your tent. When unevenly tightened, they will allow the canvas to flipflop in the wind. Couples grow apart unless they learn to communicate. And communication doesn't just happen, it requires skill and practice along with courage.

As Paul Tournier points out, "It takes courage to

face up to all the problems created by a complete adaptation of two personalities. People are very different one from another. This is a fact plain to see; yet, few will admit it, especially when it is a question of their wife or their husband. That he should have other tastes, other feelings, and other hopes is immediately reacted to as a challenge, a defiance, an attack, a rejection."[1]

ENCOURAGING CONVERSATION

If there is anything, any issue which you cannot talk to your mate about, your marriage needs a little priming in open communication. By discussing everything, a couple not only gets fully acquainted, but keeps up with each other's emotional, intellectual and spiritual growth. Circumstances don't remain static and neither do feelings and opinions.

"I don't understand men," a young wife confessed recently. "Will I ever? At home Gus is glum but let someone drop in, and he's full of humor, charm and information.

Did you ever say, "I learn more about my husband when I listen to him talk on the phone or with friends at a party?"

Before taking offense about your husband's lack of conversation, check out his home. Does his father converse freely or does his mother usually encourage the dialogue? If you are the quiet one, your husband needs to check out your family background and appreciate what he finds.

Wives often assume that husbands think their spouses are either unimportant or less intelligent.

Perhaps wives should admit that they have not learned to draw their husbands out. If you want to know what is going on in your husband's life, learn to talk about what interests him.

A woman can learn to gently probe a man with "Did you have a good lunch?" That, perhaps, will remind him about their friend he saw over lunch. Get men started, however, and they'll just talk and talk. A woman can even learn to anticipate subject areas which a man enjoys discussing.

Women generally converse more easily. This is probably so because their minds are so detailed. They need to be aware that men get tired of listening and appreciate some silence at times. Often, too, the husband has had to talk all day and prefers to rest his mind and his tongue. The wife, alone all day with the kids and eager for adult conversation, thinks only about her own needs.

Couples need to discuss, talk over, evaluate, consider, deliberate, converse, commune, banter and even argue. And, because we all change with the years, wise partners will keep abreast of the changes, both within themselves and in their relationship to one another.

Careful parents keep themselves informed on the changes — mental, social and physical — in their children. To help such parents, experts issue guides to normal behavior in children. For example, "Eleven-year-olds tend to be selfish." But astute parents know these same children at 12, 14 or 18 will be different personalities than they were at 11, because they change with the years.

Just as it is with parents and children, so it is with husbands and wives. Changes come and, if we are wise, we will note them, accept them and adjust to them. Every situation or circumstance, every new person we meet, every problem we face — both as individuals and as couples — influences some kind of change. Yet change is nothing to fear; rather it is something to anticipate.

Most of the success of mending any marriage or keeping it from becoming frayed through the inevitability of change is nothing more than husbands and wives exposing themselves to the art of healthy and honest talk about any issue or problem, even those of tremendous disagreement.

There are some basic ground rules, however, in order to keep the relationship sweet.

Use "I" Statements

"I" statements attack the situation, rather than the individual, and allow the speaker to express his or her feelings. "You" statements attack the character of the person addressed and automatically put him on the defensive. An explosive situation.

For example, the wife says, "You never fix anything around here."

Does she expect her husband to gently respond, "Now, honey, why are you so upset? What's really bothering you?" He won't.

Rather, he will defend himself with, "What about that shelf I fixed for you last Friday? You didn't even appreciate it." He's begging for appreciation.

And his own "you" statement, in turn, will stir up a defense in his wife. This kind of exchange

can continue until every former argument is rehearsed and rehashed. Conversation like this is not conducive to solving a problem and ultimately drives a wedge between mates.

Now, what if the wife would say to her husband, "I'd really like that wall fixed before my meeting next week. It's so unsightly." He would probably respond with "I'll see if I can get to it later today." Or, he will feel free to be totally honest with her and say, "I wish we could get it fixed before then. But I'm not really sure how to fix it, and anyway it's going to involve a lot of expense."

Then they can discuss without condemning each other all the problems involved in repair. In such situations, the wife holds the key to encouraging detailed, positive talk.

Eliminate Sarcasm

"Are you blind?" a wife snaps. "You just passed the turn. Now, we'll be late."

Naturally, her husband will explode in defense and yell, "No, I'm not blind. Are you helpless? You could have watched for it."

Sarcasm is a type of wit which is sharply mocking or contemptuous. Sarcastic remarks are pointedly opposite or irrelevant to the situation. Many tents are full of sarcasm. It's like having bedbugs in your sleeping bag. Very irritating.

A one-day's search for sarcasm in the home will astound you. "You're really on the ball," we remark to someone who's way behind time. "I can always count of you," we dig at the person who failed to turn on the oven.

Haim Ginott, in his *Between Parent and Teenager,* points out the danger of individuals within the family dusting off and hurling their private arsenals of instant insults at one another. Husbands and wives who cannot communicate without wielding the weapons of ridicule and invective against each other place a heavy and unnecessary burden on their marriages. Too, the use of sarcasm is always counterproductive. It only causes bitterness and invites counterattacks.

Back when Jim and I were making a point of looking for sarcasms in our vocabulary, the classic example occurred. I had run out of gas not far from home, the first time I had ever done so. Naturally, I was in a hurry and disgusted.

I rushed to a nearby phone. "Honey," I gasped, so relieved that he was home. "I ran out of gas."

I expected sympathy and emotional hospitality, but instead I got sarcasm. "You're really efficient," Jim droned. "Don't you ever look at the gas gauge?"

A horrible "you" statement! I was already frustrated. Now I was hurt, too. (Efficiency *is* one of my strong points really.) But I also had time to think before Jim came.

When he arrived with the gas can, I purposely refrained from reminding him about the times he'd run out of gas or from accusing him of not filling the tank the last time. I merely said, "I'm sorry to pull you away from your studies."

I used an "I" statement. Then I told him how his "you" statement had made me feel and how his sarcasm had hurt rather than helped.

We both gained from this experience. He learned something about my feelings and I became much more aware of the gas gauge. And it was a good lesson for us on the point of sarcasm. It gave us both a chance to put into practice talking to each other with respect and courtesy.

A good rule is "treat your mate as your best friend." After all, your mate *is* your best friend — or should be. Yet we are all guilty of treating casual acquaintances or even total strangers with more respect than we do our beloved.

Choose the Right Time

When your spouse hits the door, do you hit him with questions, bad news, bills, problems? For some husbands, coming home from work is like an obstacle course of words, kids and toys. A man can't stand confusion like a woman can. She's wise to encourage him with a hug and a chance to unwind over a glass of iced tea.

Nor is the right time to expose difference when friends or relatives are present. Yet some mates, afraid they'll not be heard, use this tactic as a lever for an embarrassed commitment or as a ploy to garner support. This is a problem found in many otherwise good tents.

Too, the husband should be sensitive to those times when his wife is particularly short-tempered or irritable, like before her period. In my case, Friday night, at the end of the work week, facing a cluttered house, is no time to bring up problems. A wife also needs to be sensitive to stress times for her husband — like taking inventory or end-of-the-month rush.

Tackle obstacles only when you know there is going to be adequate time to discuss them. Avoid discussing problems during meals or before going to bed. Jim and I make appointments to discuss serious difficulties.

Isolate Obstacles

Deal with one issue at a time. A money problem —for example, a wife's overspending on groceries —can expand to an undiscussed and unsolved problem. She counters with "What about that fishing rod you bought that you didn't talk over with me and you didn't even need." Then he can remind her about the catalog charge she didn't clear with him. And it might even evolve into "what my mother said about your mother" type of remarks. All unnecessary.

No problem is bigger than that of tackling piled-up disagreements. Make it against the rules to consider two issues at a time. It takes a little practice to stick with this rule, but it works.

Avoid Dead Issues

Leave skeletons alone. Once you've solved or uncovered the ins and outs of the fishing rod, drop it forever. When hearing words like "What about the time you...?" or "Don't forget, last year you...," one partner has to remind the other, "We solved that. Remember? It's over."

Since the wife rarely forgets anything, she can unwisely bring up old business which rekindles old fires. Make it against the rules ever to mention solved problems. Forgetting is also an art.

Be Open and Honest

"It bothers me...."

"I can't understand why you...."

Level with each other daily. When you feel something is wrong, check it out.

I'll use another personal illustration—and this will give Jim equal time! We had been making church visits and running errands much of the day. But Jim seemed cool toward me.

I couldn't put my finger on what was wrong, so I asked him, "Are you just pressured by the day, or have I done or said something to make you angry?"

"Yes, I am angry that you asked me to drive through all that traffic so you could use your bonus store coupon before it expired. Then you bought an item that you couldn't even use your coupon on. I disliked being rushed for that. I think you spent too much on earrings, too."

I was glad I asked. If I had not drawn Jim out, who knows how long that matter would have bothered him? Jim is one of those quiet ones. If the earring purchase hadn't been exposed, it could have become fuel for one of those "I didn't mention it before, but you..." flare-ups that Theodore I. Rubin writes about in *The Angry Book*.

Get rid of irritations before they become problems.

Campers can't control the weather, but they can plan to pack raincoats, books and warm clothing. An adequately prepared camper can be comfortable even in stormy weather. In the same way, open, honest and fair communication can prepare marriage partners for those stormy periods they will have to weather.

And as surely as sunshine follows the storm, so continued open and honest communication between husband and wife will lead to increased understanding. As Paul Tournier says:

"Happy are the couples who do recognize and understand that their happiness is a gift of God, who can kneel together to express their thanks not only for the love which He has put in their hearts ..., but also for the progress in their marriage which He brings about through that hard school of mutual understanding."[2]

Appreciate Your Partner

The most significant contribution to strengthening a marriage is a regular and sincere "thank you" to your mate. When he helps around the house, be sure to mention your appreciation. He'll be more inclined to help again.

The Bible says, *"Therefore all things whatsoever ye would that men should do to you, do ye even so to them* (Matthew 7:12).

If you like to be remembered on your birthday, remember him. If you appreciate an unsolicited glass of juice or water, take him one sometimes. When he does a special errand for you, like bringing gas for your empty tank, let him know you didn't just expect him to. Thank him for taking time to help.

Appreciation goes a long way and is the oil of communication. Appreciation has as its base love and respect. The Bible gives the guidelines for this kind of attitude and Jesus commanded us to love one another as He loved us. *This is my commandment, That ye love one another, as I have loved you* (John 15:12). Husbands and wives are just as bound to love each other in this way as Christians are to love fellow Christians.

Happy communication!

Footnotes

1. Paul Tournier, *To Understand Each Other* (Atlanta, Georgia: John Knox Press, 1967), p. 35.
2. Paul Tournier, *To Understand*, p. 60.

7
CAMPING TOGETHER

"The tent is up. The trenches are dug. The guy lines are tight (which has all required much work and concentration). The weather is gorgeous, so, let's take a break and do something together. Just you and me."

RECREATION

The responsibilities of marriage are so heavy and grim at times that couples should make it a rule to have some time each week for recreation together. This time must be planned for and guarded jealously in this materialistic world.

Couples are duped into collapsing in front of the television set for an uncreative night of spectatorship, when engaging in physical activity instead could release pent-up emotions and loosen

tension. I'm not talking here about having sex; I'm talking about participating in games and sports. After all, campers don't spend all their time in the tent.

Somehow, playing games together magically clears the mind. And so do sports. Try tennis, ping-pong, swimming, back-packing or whatever. Variety is good psychology. At the same time, enjoying good recreation together does brighten the sex life.

SEX

Sexual intercourse is prescribed for marriage only and wisely so. *Therefore shall a man leave his father and his mother, and shall cleave unto his wife: and they shall be one flesh. And they were both naked, the man and his wife, and were not ashamed* (Genesis

2:24). Jesus quoted from this passage when He said in Matthew 19:5, *And the twain shall be one flesh.*

Sex Outside Marriage

Unmarried couples who base marriage or love on successful sex, choosing to experiment first to see if they're compatible, often use sex as a hold on one another or demand it as proof of love. But they ignore the risks and problems involved.

For one thing, a sex life is not the same as a love life. Couples who engage in sex outside of marriage often mistake the pleasures of physical love for the kind of love that is strong enough for marriage—love based on trust. Strong and good as these sexual joys are, they tend to cool down after a while and will not carry a couple over the obstacles of marriage.

Too, sex outside of marriage may raise doubts in the mind of the partner, especially in the woman, as to whether the physical enjoyment of the body is the only attraction, rather than that of the total person.

Sex Inside Marriage

Contrary to what many people claim, sex is not a cure-all. But it is a natural, wonderful and rewarding experience for both partners.

Sex is also a barometer of sorts, for next to finances, it is the biggest cause—as well as the biggest victim—of friction between husband and wife. Let a flare-up occur in finances or in some other area which involves deep feelings, and sex is the first thing to suffer. The better things are emotionally and spiritually, the more rewarding the physical union will be.

Sex as Communion

Maxie Dunnam, writing in *Dancing at My Funeral*, reminds us that sex isn't supposed to be an act of consumption, but rather an experience of communion.

Dr. Herbert J. Miles echoes this thought by declaring, "Sexual expression in marriage is a function of the total personality at the highest and deepest levels. It makes possible tender understanding, communion and communication between husband and wife that cannot be expressed in language. Through one-flesh sexual experiences in marriage, the spiritual and the physical unite in their highest and most pleasant relationship. Husband and wife are sublimely fused into complete unity and identity through their one-flesh sexual experiences. *Truly, sex is the servant of marriage and of Christianity.*"[1]

As the Scripture says, *Let the husband render unto the wife due benevolence: and likewise also the wife unto the husband. The wife hath not power of her own body, but the husband: and likewise also the husband hath not power of his own body, but the wife* (1 Corinthians 7:3-4).

This willing kind of belonging cannot be snatched or demanded for selfish satisfaction. Intercourse is for the other's enjoyment and is a beautiful, holy experience of being one flesh.

Love-making has been compared to a worship service. It is a holy and sacred act, the most intimate of human relationships, the highest expression of love and trust. It requires work on the part of both mates.

Sex as Trust

Both mates must work at it, because love-making is not mastered quickly. Rather, it matures and grows as mutual trust and giving of each other increases and deepens.

Satisfying sex has been referred to as the 20-year warm-up. It requires patience and unselfish concern to fulfill the most intimate needs of another person.

These needs change with maturity. So good marital sex is built on trust, much like spiritual maturity demands trust and commitment to the Lord.

Sex as Understanding

Some mates will have to unlearn negative impressions regarding sex. Ideas that sex is dirty or something to be tolerated for the man's enjoyment often have to be destroyed in the mind of the wife.

Many Christians, men and women, regard sex as totally non-spiritual and having to do only with worldly pleasure. For such persons we recommend Dr. Herbert J. Miles' *Sexual Happiness in Marriage.* He does a fantastic job on this subject.[2]

And here are several pointers of our own which Jim and I have picked up from our own experience and reading which have helped other couples to find a rewarding sexual relationship.

Play fair

Don't just stand on your conjugal rights. Be fair to each other. Just as it is unfair for the husband to expect sex on demand, so it is unfair for a woman to appeal to a man's emotions and then selfishly turn him away. And it is most unfair for a woman to use sex as a lever for getting her own way or to withhold it as punishment.

Give affection

A woman is willing to give sex to get attention and a man is willing to give attention to get sex. That's the way it is. And when the husband's attentiveness to his wife is bestowed with genuine affection, results are guaranteed. For a woman wants and needs the tenderness, the caring and the caressing that her husband is equipped by God to give her before she gives herself to him.

Paul Tournier, in his book on marriage, writes about the wife's special need for affection. "The wife has an emotional need which often the husband fails to recognize. She needs to hear tender words, she needs to go out with her husband, to share excitement with him as they admire something, to experience deep oneness with him in the silence of a moment of exaltation.

"For her, love means a permanent, high level of affection. This is why she would like her husband always to be with her. She counts the hours he gives her, the Sundays he spends at home, the evenings he takes her out to the show. This is, for her, the way in which love is expressed . . . .

"Often the wife cannot experience full sexual pleasure unless sexual experience is but a part of the larger context of mutual harmony, understanding and a continuing communion in affection for one another."[3]

Say "I love you"

The wife needs to hear the words "I love you." But too often her husband thinks, "I've already told her that. She knows it."

Of course, she knows it. But she still needs to hear it — and often.

Love all day

With kind words and appreciation for each other, love play (or foreplay, as some call it) begins in the morning and continues throughout the day. What is said between 7 a.m. and 10 p.m. is more important to love-making than what is uttered in the bedroom.

Many wives resent the turned-on affection 30 minutes before sex. Why? Because the emotions of a man and woman vary greatly. A woman warms up slowly while a man warms up very quickly.

The woman is reached through her mind. Husbands should understand that it takes a while for the wife's mind to be released from all the thoughts and cares of the day and her enjoyment is directly related to her mental attitude.

So it is natural for the husband to take the lead in love-making. His touches, embraces and words prepare the woman for their physical union and create within her a longing for him. Sometimes the wife herself may want to initiate the process.

Sex as Pleasure

Intercourse can become a burden if allowed to become dull and repetitive, a physical function only. It's like sitting down to the same meal over and over. The art of love-making demands time and creativity, just as preparing an exciting menu does — a little spice here and an herb there. Any action during love play that is mutually acceptable and not offensive to the other is proper.

Conveying to the other partner that you are looking forward to the physical union by a whispered hint, a special touch or look, a burning candle or soft music, will add a note of excitement and an air of expectancy. Anticipation is half the enjoyment.

It behooves couples interested in keeping this vital part of marriage alive to be continually learning all they can.

Footnote

1. Herbert J. Miles, *Sexual Happiness in Marriage* (Grand Rapids, Michigan: Zondervan Publishing House, 1967), p. 38.
2. Dr. Miles does an equally fine job on a number of other points which Jim and I have learned through experience — a slow process. Where was Dr. Miles when we needed him 23 years ago?
3. Paul Tournier, *To Understand Each Other* (Atlanta, Georgia: John Knox Press, 1967), p. 45.

8

THE CONTENTED CAMPER

THE late Peter Marshall, in *A Man Called Peter*, referred to marriage as the halls of highest human happiness. And so it is. But happiness doesn't just happen. Nor does romance survive in a vacuum.

Couples who have found happiness in their tents and who have kept romance alive in their marriages will tell you that it was no accident. A lot of work supported by a great deal of encouragement went into getting those tents up and keeping them mended.

Marriages, like people, go through stages and changes: childhood, adolescence and maturity. Attitudes change with regard to financial pressures, to children who come and go, to retirement needs. Every place a couple lives, every friend they come to know and every job they have produces new challenges and problems of adjustment. The uncertainties of tragedy, illness and loss of loved ones require special understanding and patience, since each experience exposes new characteristics and old fears.

So the mending of a marriage goes on and on, aided especially by the wife's special gift of encouragement. This mending and reinforcement can become as enjoyable and satisfying a venture as putting up the tent in the first place.

First Corinthians 13:4-8 (*NASB*) sets a very high, but obtainable standard for love:

Love is patient, love is kind, and is not jealous; love does not brag and is not arrogant, does not act unbecomingly; it does not seek its own, is not provoked, does not take into account a wrong suffered, does not rejoice in unrighteousness, but rejoices with the truth; bears all things, believes all things, hopes all things, endures all things.

Love never fails.

When a husband and wife are committed personally to Jesus and love each other this way, they can expect not only a fulfilling marriage, but can say with complete confidence from the very beginning, "Only death could ever part us."

There are many beautiful and sturdy tents around. They have endured many storms and provided havens for numberless campers. Some have been patched and sewn many times. But from a distance, we don't even notice the mended places.

Sharing a life together is never simple. Yet the effort is worth all it costs, for a good marriage is priceless. And what could be worth more than that?

Paul Tournier, again, says it better than I could: "Marriage then becomes a great adventure, a continuous discovery both of oneself and one's mate. It becomes a daily broadening of one's horizon, an opportunity of learning something new about life, about human existence, about God. This is why in the beginning of the Bible God says, *It is not good that man should be alone.*"[1]

Happy tenting to you both!

Footnotes

1. Paul Tournier, *To Understand Each Other* (Atlanta, Georgia: John Knox Press, 1967), p. 30.

BIBLIOGRAPHY

Ginott, Haim. *Between Parent and Teenager.* New York: Macmillan Publishing Co., 1969.

Hendricks, Howard G. *Heaven Help the Home!* Wheaton, Illinois: Victor Books, 1974.

Mace, David and Vera. *How to Have a Happy Marriage.* Nashville, Tennessee: Abingdon Press, 1977.

Marshall, Catherine. *A Man Called Peter.* New York: McGraw-Hill Book Co., 1951.

Marshall, Peter. *John Doe, Disciple: Sermons for the Young.* New York: McGraw-Hill Book Co., 1963.

Miles, Herbert J., Ph.D. *Sexual Happiness in Marriage.* Grand Rapids, Michigan: Zondervan Publishing House, 1967.

Osborne, Cecil G. *The Art of Learning to Love Yourself.* Grand Rapids, Michigan: Zondervan Corporation, 1976.

Shedd, Charlie. *Letters to Karen: On Keeping Love in Marriage.* Nashville, Tennessee: Abingdon Press, 1965.

Shedd, Charlie. *Letters to Philip: On How to Treat a Woman.* New York: Doubleday & Co., 1968.

Tournier, Paul. *To Understand Each Other.* Atlanta, Georgia: John Knox Press, 1967.

Tournier, Paul. *The Meaning of Persons.* New York: Harper and Row, 1957.

Webb, Lance. *Discovering Love.* Nashville, Tennessee: Abingdon Press, 1946.